Gathering Stones

Gathering Stones

KB Ballentine

Knoxville, Tennessee

Celtic Cat Publishing
2654 Wild Fern Lane
Knoxville, Tennessee 37931
www.celticcatpublishing.com

Manufactured in the United States of America
Design by Greyhound Books
Cover photograph by Jim Johnston

We look forward to hearing from you. Please send comments about this book to the publisher at the address above. For information about special educational discounts and discounts for bulk purchases, please contact Celtic Cat Publishing.

Acknowledgements: “Coal, Inc.” was previously published in the 2007 Spring edition of *Touchstone*. The author was a recipient of the *Dorothy Sargent Rosenberg Memorial Fund* Award 2007 for her poem “Midsummer’s Eve.”

ISBN: 978-0-9658950-9-5

Library of Congress Control Number: 2007940743

For those whose voices were never heard
and CKA whose belief never wavered

Though I should mingle with the dust, or fall to ashes in flame, the plough will always remain to furrow the earth, the stars will always be there to unveil the beauty of the night, and a newer people, living a newer life, will sing like the sons of the morning.

– Sean O'Casey

Table of Contents

A Time to Speak

A Time to Die

A Time to Dance

Acknowledgements

Many people have helped me on this journey, and it would be remiss of me not to acknowledge their contribution to my work. To the Craft of Writing group – my MFA buddies who constantly supported and encouraged my work: Caitlin Krause, Joyce Johnson, Michelle Parnett, Jodi Dougherty, Dianna Calaruso, Karon Powell, and Kelly Harris. To my professors and mentors at Lesley University's MFA in Creative Writing program for endeavoring to make my writing the best they knew it could be: Steven Cramer, Teresa Cader, Janet Sylvester, and Don Share. To Penny Dyer, Helga Kidder, Finn Bille, and John Mannone – tireless workers in the art of creating poems; my workshop groups at the Chattanooga Writers' Guild, Rhyme-n-Chatt, and Tennessee Mountain Writers, Inc. for encouraging writing participation. To my monthly Open Mic group who listened tirelessly to several versions of these poems. And to the various friends who have made this book possible: Kenny Allred, Kristi Walker, Jeff Ferrell, Janie Sheldon, Jessie Lendennie, John Fields, and Valerie Cannon. To my family for their unconditional love. Much love and gratitude to all of you.

Author's Foreword

Have you ever been to a place so breathtaking an emotional well-spring rises that makes it literally hurt to view it? I have – on the western coast of that little green rock known as Ireland, Erin, Rosaleen, Éire.

Many names to match her many qualities – terrifying and lovely, serene and turmoiled; a land peopled by warriors and druids, farmers and fishermen, commoners and kings. Then there are the Others – the Little People of folklore and legend, and the stones that have existed since before time began – they, too, have a story to tell.

From the cities of the North and East to the moonscape of the Burren stepping out to the Aran Islands in the West, Ireland is an island of voices – each yearning to be heard. Not to the exclusion of the others, but in addition to them – a chorus, a joining of spirits across the ages.

And voices answer across the ocean, each heartbeat echoes the pounding surf, its depths as beyond reach as the past. For every coastal town that saw her children leave for a better life, for each field filled with the blood of her youth, there has been a homecoming. A few generations after many families left Ireland for the hope of a better life – or at least a life – her children are returning.

Gathering Stones will take you on a journey of Ireland's past through her turbulent history and into her promising future. Gather stones of new memory as you read, a better vision of what she can become. Between wisps of fog and watery sun, blue peeks again and pinpricks of silver shimmer across the sea.

Publisher's Preface

To every thing there is a season . . . a time to cast away stones, and a time to gather stones together. . .

—Ecclesiastes 3

I first met Karie (KB) in 1997. She had begun to unearth the stones of her past. Upon returning from her first visit to Ireland, she had written to me hoping that I could provide her with a deeper understanding of the history of Northern Ireland and the Troubles in particular.

Since that initial contact, we have met at various workshops and readings. I have watched with great pleasure the growth in KB's writing, a growth recognized by others in the form of literary awards and publication of her work.

KB has returned to Ireland on many occasions since 1997, so it is perhaps not surprising that her first collection of poems is inspired by the many stones she has collected during her ancestral search.

Stones are shaped over time . . . from the slow movement of ice fields to the fast flowing water of rivers and streams. *Gathering Stones* is a trilogy through time. In "A Time to Speak", KB introduces us to the phantoms, faeries, and folklore that first influenced her reading and fascination with Ireland. For the most part, such stories passed through the spoken word from one generation to another.

The second section of *Gathering Stones* moves away from folklore to reality as KB poignantly explores the more unsettled periods of Irish history – the many occupations, the struggles for freedom, the Great Famine of the nineteenth century and its legacy on America, and the more recent Troubles in Northern Ireland. For millions in Ireland, it was “A Time to Die”.

The concluding segment focuses on the beauty of Ireland, the Ireland that most people think of — the forty shades of green, the coastal cliffs, the narrow twisting roads, the large stone castles, the islands off the west coast, the peat fires and pubs, and the friendliness of people who love nothing better than the return of a distant family member, even if it is only a “quick wee visit.” “A Time to Dance” celebrates KB’s triumphant journey of self-discovery to her ancestral home.

Today, approximately forty-four million Americans trace their roots back to Ireland. For so many, including me, the impetus to emigrate was the desire to escape the killing and conflict that has plagued Ireland for centuries. For many, emigration was driven by a grinding poverty and ceaseless oppression. For some, America simply offered the opportunity of a better life. Whatever the reason, most Irish-Americans have a deep love of Ireland and a lasting pride in their Irish heritage. KB once shared with me that when she got off the bus at the Cliffs of Moher, a jolt went all the way through her body. She knew she was home.

As we begin this journey with KB, my hope is that we may gather stones together.

Jim Johnston
Publisher
Celtic Cat Publishing

A Time to Speak

Gathering Stones

3

Renaming the Dark

Yesterday I dared to struggle, today I dared to win.
– Bernadette Davies

Sometimes sorrow comes suddenly
like a sparrow taking flight as you hike
by her nest in the shaded wood

or creeps in like mist that rolls up
from the sea, seeping into everything,
leaving you saturated, still asleep
and surrounded by fog.

How could you know
that a fork in the road would change the life
you anticipated? Why hold on when letting go
could have saved you both?

A blackbird rises in the mist. You have not
passed this way before. Though often silent,
the dead don't lie when they speak.

And they do speak.

And they do speak.

Hebrides

There is a Hebridean silence . . . it is a total, peaceful serenity broken only by birdsong or the lapping of the waves . . .
— Mark Shorrock

Circled stones rise from the island's center.
Ruined might silent under September sun,
they glitter with salted surf,
besieged, unconquered.

Choughs chatter above the spuming foam.
Sea oats bow into tawny arches
shuddering the sand under a sky
as wide as the sea.

Sanctuary no longer heralded by man
– a transient kind of power.

Kerry

Ana's paps once gave life to this land.
Salmon leapt upriver and red deer
nuzzled the banks. Silver birch peered
through aspens as they whispered
in the wind, hazel loitering beneath.

As the sun skims low and mist mounts,
go with the faeries, wander the woods
no longer there – watch Caer shift from swan
to maid as Oenghus declares his love, witness
Diarmaid's disgrace and boar-ish death,
Etain's life as woman, water, worm, butterfly –
ficheall piece of *sí* and man.

Awake now, vision clear, walk the way of Éire.

The Siren's Song

Curlews and gulls carve the wind and land on rocky ledges,
sheltered from the gusts that shock your tar and timber haven.
Above, the blue for you has resolved to gray, threatening.
Wavelets rough the sea's surface, lobster boats plying for Cárna's shore.

Sheltered from the gusts that shock your tar and timber haven,
I hear your shouts, a tinny sound among the snarl of surf.
Wavelets rough the sea's surface, lobster boats plying for Cárna's shore
as I watch from swirling water, roll with each surge, revel in the danger.

I hear your shouts, a tinny sound among the snarl of surf;
you left it too late, too far out. Boards splinter and crack.
I watch from swirling water, roll with each surge, revel in the danger,
waves trampling toward the stony coast, gritty with salt.

You left it too late, too far out. Boards splinter and crack.
My world vibrates in constant rhythm with the heaving tide,
waves trampling toward the stony coast, gritty with salt.
My scales reflect rainbows on rock-ribbed reefs and pulsing kelp.

My world vibrates in constant rhythm with the heaving tide.
The cold, the stinging salt soak your lungs as you enter my liquid chamber,
my scales reflecting rainbows on rock-ribbed reefs and pulsing kelp,
my embrace as rimy as the sea that surrounds you.

The cold, the stinging salt soak your lungs as you enter my liquid chamber
– bubbles suspend, cease to rise as we descend to my grainy bed.
My embrace is as rimy as the sea that surrounds you;
I will lay you down beside the others until currents summon me to the surfac

Bubbles suspend, cease to rise as we descend to our grainy bed.
Above, the blue for you has resolved to grey, threatening.
I will lay you down beside the others until currents summon me to the surfac
when curlews and gulls carve the wind and land on rocky ledges.

Sacrifice

Stone sentinels touched
the midnight sky, cast
shadows over the moonlit
meadow. Phantoms faded
in and out of darkness,
floated around the circle,
caressed each granite.
Silence
so thick it pressed
my skin, wrapped
around and choked me.
Cold seeped through my robe
from my rocky bed, and stars
glared into my staring eyes.
Fascinated, terrified,
unable to cry out,
I watched. Whispers
of cloth rustled close,
and a hooded figure
drew near. A cloaked arm
rose like the crescent moon,
and a sliver of silver flashed.

Stillness
floats over the field.
Sunrise breaks
along the horizon,
and waking birds quiver
among the trees.
Weathered stones reveal
no secret, rooted and mute
as ancient sentries. Only
a dark patch within
the ring, and the faint smell
of rust in the dew.

Winter Solstice at Newgrange

Past the ring of granite
darkness surrounds, cool
air creeps along the stones
awakening memories. Men
hewed and carried this rock,
shaped this passage, waited

to welcome the sun.

Inside this hollow hill,
three days bring rebirth –
Celtic knots spiral, ripple
with light. The world stirs,
unfurls.

Midsummer's Eve

The firefly lights the wild hare's eye and to the north
the white door opens under bare Ben Bulben.

Darkness inks all corners of the sky, light scuttling
for cover, resurfacing with the pale round moon.

Hayricks burgeon in fields as rowans fade,
summer growth waning. Wind rustles the musky

night, and ribbons of fog stretch into vapor. Ashen
and ghostly, a barn owl blunders across the horizon.

Toads nudge from mud baked by the sun's rays and croak a bass
to the crickets' hum; Carolan's harp couldn't compose such a tune.

This is the night old dames gather herbs to store
for *samhain*, when frost hoars the hardening earth;

this is the night when girls on the cusp of womanhood long
for a chance to dance with the king of the faeries.

The moon fades as daybreak lavenders the sky; crickets and toads
grow quiet while a doe and her fawn stir the mist across the woodline.

Dawn shimmers and approaches, shadows tarry at the base
of Ben Bulben and the white door closes once more.

Brú na Bóinne

Drawn from the dark, the secret
places, tranquil water welcomes
the hazel husk, closes slowly around
and over it, rippling out to where
the stream gushes and flows. The shade
of these seven trees leaves the grass wet
with dew long after noon, yet tufts spring
up in lush masses all around the bank,
clover clinging to the gentle slopes.
Air still and thick drowses those who
would enter here – Bóann urges them
to drink, drink deeply of this place – makes
them dream of the beginning and the end
of time. They wake to the voice of the river.

Holy Well

Once revered, even feared,
this ancient spring bubbles
with life, though centuries
have run away with all but
weathered stones and nettles.

circle once face the rising sun,
even through falling rain

Don't try to understand
just accept by faith, trust
this pool of holy water.
Unseen fount, forever refreshing,
forever cleansing itself.

circle twice and cross your heart

Look around, miles of space
graced with butterwort, chamomile.
Don't be afraid to walk this path,
take this course, your voice loud
in the silence.

third time around kneel on the ground,
an attitude of prayer

Offer your coin, your cloth, yourself.
Remember those who used to believe.

Elm & Ash & Oak

Ailim be the lady's tree; burn it not
or cursed ye'll be.
– Rudyard Kipling

Out of the fire
desire for success;
feed on others or be devoured.
Dancing light heightens need.
Wood, turf pops with heat, propels up and on.

Out of the ash
what remains?
Stubble, fragments –
whatever could survive the flame, stronger
by refining white hot judgment.

Out of the dust
what will stand?
An orgy of hope
showers fields with eternal grains joining
their brothers, kindling existence again.

Decorating the Holy Tree on Feast Day

Beloved, gaze in thine own heart,
The holy tree is growing there
– WB Yeats

Barren arms thrust into blue-gray
skies, an exposed skeleton
feared, revered, alone most of the year.
White blossoms begin to bud,
flesh the knobby, thorny bones.

With dew soaked feet,
pilgrims, petitioners bear offerings, pleas.
Like sap oozing from a severed flower,
the procession trickles then swells,
abrades the path once muscled with grass.

One by one the bony arms fill, tied
with cloth and string and prayer.

No longer shunned, hawthorn bends
above the circle of well wishers chanting
over a chorus of starlings. The sun vaults
the horizon, kaleidoscopes around
blossoms and ribbons waving at the center
of an extending, pulsing ring.

Redemption

Mists from the west shroud the Golden Shore.
In fact, I've never seen it, not really.
Just shimmers after a rain or as sun sighs
into the ocean at day's end. Green hills undulating
at my back while white-bearded waves wash my feet
seem so like Paradise, what more could *Tír na Nóg* offer?

So many tides have turned since childhood's innocence,
like pixie dust and pots of gold, I forget to look
for the Golden Shore. I've lost myself somewhere
along the way. The world claims all effort, consciousness.
But as daylight melts into moonlight, I peer into my daughter's
eyes, smooth my son's cowlick as he struggles with sleep –

they still believe.

Celtic Seasonal

In the east the sky purples and mists,
gentles over budding green. Lengthening
days remind us sowing soon will follow.

Under the white noon, southerly breezes
harp a tune. Energy pulses – quickens,
blesses life growing in the earth.

Dusk darkens the land, and the wise learn
to let go. Leaves tarnish then drift, like wisdom,
into gathering gloom, mutter in baring branches.

Midnight approaches. North wind challenges
starlight, obliterating hope. Cold pinpricks
sweep east where the future begins.

Brigid

St Brigid
heal us
we pray,
come to
our aid.
Paper, ribbon, twine, picture,
candle, coin—tokens of lives
needing your touch. Kneel in
the cool
quiet tun-
nel. Dip
fingers in
still water.
Sign the
c r o s s.
Make an
o f f e r ing.
B e l i e v e.

And they do speak.

Gathering Stones

A Time to Die

Valley of Dry Bones

—Ezekiel 37

Rise up, oh, my brothers, rise up!

The sun still beats like our neighbor's steel
fist, and though your bodies have turned
to dust your fight is not forgotten.

Your blood flows through this land,
and this land is in my blood –
we are one and forever the same.

River and wind harmonize a nameless tune
of faeries and battles, cascade through my mind.
The slow sob of sea on shore ceaselessly echoes

the sobs of the hungry, the ill, the poor
from a lifetime ago. A lifetime – yours – and still
our people suffer. Mine – and still the anger roils.

Rise up, oh, my brothers, rise up!

Out of the North

The Vikings, unlike the Romans before them, did not spare Ireland. During the ninth & tenth centuries, waves of Norse warriors ransacked the countryside. The Vikings plundered everything in sight.

—Earthlore

My story begins in another country
where eyes fear every night sky,
where wind screams high on the hillside,
a place where innocence dies.

Once this valley was fertile and green,
once the sun shone cool and fair,
but invaders raided the valley,
stripped it – left it bleeding and bare.

They slaughtered the stock, killed the men
oblivious to children's cries;
divided the living from the dead,
parted mam and babe with no goodbyes.

Burned out shells are the only remains
of homes and hearths once tended with care.
A canopy of gray stretches over
blackened crops, land echoing despair.

Bird and bloom should rise from the earth,
but no voice disturbs this scene.
Time reclaims the ashy sod as lakes
heave under brooding trees.

My story begins in another country
where no eyes breach the night skies,
where wind screams high on the hillside.
A place where innocence died.

Gráinne

The moon-tide sea murmurs. Gráinne
sways to its ebb and flow on the creaking
boards. All quiet, clouds scud the moon.
Men asleep, this is her favorite
time – slap and suck of waves on wood,
snores, cool wind sighing through the night.

She rubs her hand against her neck, hair tangling
in the wind – loose after a day spent tightly coiled.
Gráinne grins, thinking of the gold below. Taken
from the English unable to slip past this coast –
her coast – at the fortune of flood and tide.

Here is peace. Far away from carts and dogs
and cities, far away from farmers digging
their lives away. Life is in each foamy
wave rolling over the black ocean, heart
beating to its rhythm.

Pirate Queen of Connaught
Gráinne Ní Mhaille

1.

Hair like flame against brilliant blue
of sea and sky wasn't difficult to spot.
There she was again, among the men
bustling on boats. The mother sighed,
despaired of making her daughter a lady.

2.

Like wool drenched with ink, clouds
hung heavy on the horizon, familiar mist
dampened the canvas where fighting churned
on deck. From below, Gráinne watched
her father's men battle the English. Screams
pricked the thick air, and she climbed on deck,
spied her father, weapon out of reach, facing
a grinning attacker. She launched on the man.
Her father seized his knife and found the other
man's gut, forever removing his grin, tide turning.

3.

Waves galloped across the ocean, black clouds piled
atop each other – Gráinne turned the prow toward
the islands trying to out-race the storm. Wind and rain
tossed the boat, but the sea in the bay bucked only
a little – a familiar feel. Husband somewhere on land,
Gráinne thrived on the challenge – fed their people,
stretched their borders – feet steadiest on water.
The crew settled to outwait the squall, sea-horse and lion
streaming from the mastheads, eager for the sea.

4.

The tide told her it was time to leave. Husband dead,
whispered as the Dark Lady of Doona for killing
her lover's murderers, Gráinne felt the changing wind
and would wed her dead husband's nephew. This marriage
gave her control of the bay and a castle to boot. What more
could she want? She turned her eyes to the sea, heard
the gulls cry. Her groom waited on the other side of the wall.

5.

Three times mother already, birth at sea even better.
Lulled by swaying waves, rest next day disturbed
by pirates. On her coast? The Irish routed them as
Gráinne left babe below, dashed on deck. No contest.
The sea-queen sailed home with unexpected birthday spoils.

6.

Five castles and the waves at her command, Gráinne raided
foreigners on her coast. Arrested, betrayed by one son,
another murdered, not even English laws changed her ways.
Practice wrangling with chieftains and governors, she sailed
to Greenwich, petitioned the queen, held her lands.

7.

Always her own mistress, she bowed only to the spray of salt
and splashing tide, wind and sea running through her blood.
The ocean, that rolling wilderness, beat in her heart, rhythm
throbbing a constant refrain, a pulse that never dies.

Warps and Wefts

After seeing your land and family rot
away, how do you pick up the threads
of your life? What pattern is left to weave
when all you can imagine is a blanket
of blackness? You don't remember
the last time you were happy – just that it was
before the fog: fog that brought death swifter
than last breath. A breath, just one. That's all
you could take after crops turned blacker
than soil, after the last moldy potato was gone.
After days lengthened into one long hungry night
with no dawn in sight. One by one the unweaving
began, and the threads that colored your world
blew away, leaving you cold and alone.

An Górta Mór

And the sea will grant each man new hope.
– Christopher Columbus

1847.
Cloudless skies wheel
over waves of green hills.
No eyes on the congested
dock regard the splendor,
already gazing toward a new
horizon . . . . No noise
from the crowd, lined up
as those already dead,
rumbling stomachs gnaw
in wasted bodies – pressing
toward the coffin ship
to make this their last gamble.
Those too tired, too old, too
stubborn to leave wave
farewell, despair flooding
where families had huddled.

1847.
Farther north on the same coast, the same sky drapes
another dock – one swarming with life. Men greet
and curse each other, children scramble across slimy
boards playing, shouting. Dock workers load bushels
and boxes of peas, beans, salmon onto one ship while others
herd cattle up the planks of another, both headed east
across the Irish Sea. A thousand gallons of liquid grain
barreled into rows wait for the next British-bound ship.

1847.
Silence from across the sea.
Thousands of my Irish brothers
and sisters starve.

Stone Voices

Snow sweeps the threshold,
door long gone for fuel, food.
A boy, a girl – who can tell? –
lies alone, without a sound,
looking into the night, no fire
to warm or light. Waiting,
listening to the stones, natives
outlasting memory.

Dawn carries voices, brings
the bailiff to tear the hovel.
Men clear the area, fighting
new flakes – find the snow-
wrapped child, eyes open,
stones listening for a breath.

Gathering Stones

Searching by moonlight, scouring by day,
rough hands find rock, dirt, straw. Babes
wail awhile then remain silent.

clear the fields, boys, clear the fields,
soup's waitin' when you're through

Bloated bodies with grass-stained mouths
linger beside the road, none strong enough
to bury the dead.

clear the fields, boys, clear the fields,
bread's waitin' when you're through

Leave hills, home, swap rocks for a sack
full of scraps, nothing left but the journey.

clear the fields, boys, clear the fields,
God's waitin' when you're through

Patrimony

Our scalpeen stands, ugly and tremulous, as frail as morning
fog hovering fields, lingering to greet the sun, when even nettles
glisten. Quilts and flour sacks flap the broken boards, muttering.
The kitchen bench perches near a frugal flame open to the sky.

The landlord won't work this land, his deeded, unloved earth. No
blood or sweat for him, instead he hires agents to tear our home.
No more songs over these fields, this bit will be left to sheep, cows
– we, less than animals, make way for them – God help us.

My grandfather tilled this soil with a skinny mule, built the fence
the agents smashed; Gran planted the potatoes we have gathered
year after year. The skeleton of their house surrounds us, everything
scattered. Sideways stands the bed my mother was born in, I was born

in, our babies were born in, protects us from the wind. So our
scalpeen stands, for now, our name our only monument.

Macroom, County Cork 1847

Quietly she digs.
No one must see
there are no coffins,
no priest, only one
mourner.
She clutches
her sore stomach.
Nothing stirs.
The moon rises,
pale as a corpse.
One last touch –
remembering
Sean chasing
the cat, Brian
wiping jam
on Nora Callan's
dress, baby
Kathleen's
hungry gurgle –
not these shriveled,
gray shapes. Uprooting
clumps of grass,
clay mounds,
she lays their bodies
into the earth.
A kiss for each
forehead.
She packs the soil
over brown trousers,
pink blanket,
her handprints the only
tribute.
She makes the sign
of the cross
then stretches on top
of the earth. Already
her body belongs.

Rosaleen's Dark Harbor

Silence lords this land beside the sea
where seals dive the shallows and men fish the deep.

Cut turf bakes into peat waiting its turn
in the fire. And the cycle continues ad infinitum.

A misty genesis of trees and harvest,
only the rocks remain, proclaim new history –

mounds of stone, messages lost to symbol and myth, time.
Headstones guard those who fell against enemies, against herself.

The final revelation is there is no *Tír na Nóg*.
No matter how green the field, gray markers aren't far away,

no matter how bright the sun, the rain still falls.
We dream of another place, resign ourselves to leaving this one.

Silent Night

As always, daylight fades into darkness.
Stars pop into the sky and a waiting
hush fills the frosted fields.
A picture postcard night.

Silence
deeper than snow
engulfs the land that
last year rang with laughter.
Huddled in a hovel, a family waits
their fate.
Not all in the mass of thin limbs
and huge eyes are still alive, but who
can carry Gran to a decent grave?
Who can pull the shriveled babe from
his mother's arms?

Long after the potato fog
after the wailing
after the begging
came the quiet.
Graveyard nettles and unwary rats
fed families until only
grass and stones,
bodies
          and
silence
are left.

Before the Crossing

The waves are old, so very old, turning tides incessantly.
Once more day has dawned in gray, no light in heaven's sky
and from my slumbering, dreamless sleep awakens me.

The sea reflects its bleakness as the water rises high,
and curraghs won't go out today for death it lingers near.
The waves are old, so very old, turning tides incessantly.

Clouds growl low on horizon's end and white foam flies
while barefoot children watch with hungry, haunted eyes.
From my slumbering, dreamless sleep they awaken me.

Feeble fires burn, every cottage echoes with babies' longing cries;
food runs low, spuds won't grow, and all are filled with fear.
The waves are old, so very old, turning tides incessantly.

Rock expands, fields shrink, beach stripped of all but sand;
rain spatters then pours as men and women starve and sigh,
and from my slumbering, dreamless sleep awaken me.

The swell grows cold and washes me from this door, pounds
upon a different, distant shore where a new world waits.
The waves are old, so very old, turning tides incessantly,
and from my slumbering, dreamless sleep awaken me.

Titanic

A quiet night
a drifting berg
a speeding ship

collision course
with death.

Icy, water shivers
down the spine
roiling
rushing
filling ears.

Frigid fingers
tug the foot
grip the neck.

Fear personified
God deified.

Breathe
a silent prayer –

salvation.

In Memoriam: Padraig Pearse

Resurrection should follow the Easter
grave but instead of rising, some are just
remembered.

– His ghost lingers by the columns
of Dublin's General Post Office,
a perennial shade playing cat-and-mouse
with those who have the right vision –
who peer into Ireland's past,
trace the fury of bullets chipped
into stone walls, envisage the men
who battled here, whose executions
electrified a nation.

Etched in granite, names once scribbled
on paper still tremble the air:
It's not over yet.

Beal na mBlath

The Twelve Apostles delivered their bouquets
of bullets and bombs, and Collins signed
the bill. Irish love dispatched these directly
to the head, the heart – a gift. The world
disordered, all that went before like petals
scattered by the wind.

Uninvited, ignoring the Lord's
day, the enemy rolled onto the playing field to toss
their own spray at anyone who could catch them,
and twelve did. The struggle brought new fodder
to the fight. The Big Fella tried to make it right,
but in the safety of home, at the mouth of flowers,

a bouquet was delivered to him.

Time Wrinkle

The gloaming deepens, darkens,
grows cold. Staring into the sky,
the stargazer's mind wanders
far from British Belfast back
to Celtic crosses and beyond –
nights entrenched in bonfire light,
pastures aglow and faces mesmerized
with delight – days, weeks, months
of labor left behind.
The bodhrán
thumps in his blood, brings his thoughts
back to the fields filled with phantoms
in rhythm with his soul.

A Pot of Gold

To be Irish is to know that in the end the world will break your heart.
– Daniel Patrick Moynihan

Oh, the luck of the Irish
on this St Paddy's Day;
another bomb went off
along MacGregor's Way.

The Protestants sport orange,
and Catholics wear the green,
fallen bodies wrapped with red;
colors merge into a dream –

a dream they share
to meld their colors true;
a nightmare now as one
more family pays its due.

Oh, for the bright orange glow of a Mayo morn
and the song of a curlew's cry.
Oh, for the green of a Kerry field
and the peace of a cloudless sky.

Under the shadow of the Mournes,
brother fights against brother,
and in Belfast silence follows sirens
as one man kills another.

Neighbors dodge, the bullets fly,
like thundering hail they pour.
Hope and love and life
lost in the grime and gore.

See your mothers, your daughters:
why let them suffer this pain?
What about it, you ask,
we're reliving the sin of Cain.

Lessons in Ardoyne

What began as a . . . row over access to Ardoyne's Catholic Holy Cross School . . . took a step over the edge today when loyalist paramilitaries terrorized little girls as young as four with a bomb attack. . . . [J]eers came from the crowd of men, followed by stones and small pieces of paving.

– BBC News, September 2001

The walk seems long but school's prepared
across cement and barbed wire fences. Do
we dare face this truth that hate abounds?
One more heart-sore family sews a shroud.

Fresh-pressed jumpers, pigtails nod around faces
keen to learn; little girl excitement rudely
erased – sun vanishes beyond fire and smoke,
a hailstorm of pavement and bottles broken,

sprays upon cars and children alike,
graffiti and curses not potent enough a strike.
Bounded by walls and mounting stone markers,
visions of revenge twist into actions darker.

What do we do, caught in this snare,
a nation's sin and shame now laid bare?
This smoldering anger rots and corrupts;
it maims and destroys but never will rust.

Holy Cross meant to fuel learning fodder;
our daughters, instead, led into slaughter.
Giggles transformed to a scream's ghastly sound,
who will go home and who under ground?

And they do speak.

Ensnared

How do we keep the peace when hate
crawls, sneaks into souls waiting
at the crossroads?

The city waits
at either end. Apprehension, hope vibrate
the air as Belfast holds her breath.

Cease-fire. But there's always one –
Where does it end? we wonder.
Where's reason? Maybe we killed that, too.

Forsaking Shiloh

(for Northern Ireland)

—Psalm 78:58-64

The dead wink
at me across the city
wall – a mirage from not
so long ago. Do I cross
into this land of despair?

Cradle to grave
we destroy each other:

accuse government,
blame God,
condemn everyone
except those who
hurl the rock,
aim the knife,
throw the bottle,
engage the trigger.

We live in hazy hate,
secrets of our souls
locked inside our hearts.
No one really trusts
peace will come.

Harboring hope makes living
more dear. I cross the wall,
breathe out resistance.

Gathering Stones

A Time to Dance

And they do speak.

Between Two Worlds

Freedom's just another word for nothin' left to lose.
—Janis Joplin

The boistrous blood of my homeland
beats forever in my veins. Like oceans
crashing a rocky shore, I am consumed,
restless for the music and spirit of my ancestors.

Leaving poverty-stricken, English-invaded soil
for more unromantic gain, my gran folded her girlish
dreams and left behind grassy fields dotted with *sidhe*
to begin a new life where no faeries lived. 'Tis said
those who cross the ocean may change their sky,
but not their soul, and Gran could not change hers.

In language that rose and fell like the never-ceasing
waves, her stories snared me in some half-remembered
dream, held me captive like the Fomorians in her bedtime
stories. Her Gaelic tongue flowed with tales but calloused
when she recalled all she'd given up.

But, Gran, I would say, *didn't coming here make you free?*

She'd pat my cheek, *'Tis grand now, to be sure. But 'tisn't grand*
to be free when you must make your own way in the world
without money, without land, without friends.

Then why'd you leave Ireland, Gran?

Ahh, she'd say, eyes focused on something I couldn't see.
Sure, 'tisn't grand when a wee bit o' bread is wealth
and no one imagines tomorrow, much less next week.

And a sorrow I could never understand, would never
understand, stretched between us, and the chill of sea
pirates chased the waves throbbing in my veins.

The Starving Time

My gran refuses to speak of it,
as though it never happened –
silence denying fact?

She lost all on the rocks of home,
an island of ready-made gravestones
spreading over fields,

like the blighted fog that took
everything. A lovely place now,
I've heard, though not from Gran.

She doesn't talk of the Old Country
at all, at all – the land where Roísín,
Malachy, and baby Liam lie, sleeping

through the ages. Ages when Gran
made it to new shores, where life
began again and death must be
forgot.

At least that kind of death. Hush.
A land of graves stretches across
ocean, time.

Coal, Inc.

His parents sailed from rock-
filled island to survive. To survive,
my father plunged into rocks
and knew only darkness.
Six of seven days he'd swelter
in the belly of the earth,
enclosed by dirt and rock,
covered with coal dust that soaked
into the skin,
        the soul.
Coal that bled from the inside
                    out and stained
the surrounding hills with rust.

At night he rocked
the baby's cradle with blackened
hands and after supper settled
in with sour mash.
                    Each morning
I rose to the smell of biscuits baking
on a stove he'd already stoked and fired;
Momma's stained apron fluttered
in her haste to get him out the door before
the whistle blew.

                    Once, he told me
he imagined the mine's blackness
was shade cast by giant oaks
and every man's lamp a persimmon
waiting to be picked. That's how he made it
till the end of shift, when he'd wind his way
through the jagged maze of rocks
ready to tear a man's hands,
                    like thorns in a briar patch,
and stagger into the fading sun.

American Heritage

My ethnic voice has been silenced by the blanket term *white.*

Born of Americans born of Americans born of travelers on the sea . . .
My heritage lies across the vast ocean on the stony
shores of ancient Ireland and on Scotland's misted moors.

I hail from the lands of Aran sweaters and tartans,
fishermen and warriors. The call of the Celt is in my blood –
voice of bards, strength of farmers, grace of dancers.
Twin cords of religion and superstition run through my veins.

Born of Americans born of Americans born of pilgrims over the sea . . .

In another life stars swathe a field of stone. Whimpers
of the dying struggling for the last potato peel, the last crumb,
drift through the night air, rustle the tangled bracken.

The only light rioting the night blazes from a plantation house
where music and laughter conceal an Irish mother dead on an English doorstep.
The Great Famine,
the Mass Emigration
has begun.

Born of Americans born of Americans born of voyagers over the waters . . .

On the dark side of the moon, vapor and moor converge
in a field of plaid. Crushed heather floats like perfume,
doesn't cover the stench of death. Clanging and clashing split
the surrounding mountainside. Scots wielding broadswords
and targes will win or die by growls and steel.
No cries for mercy,
no pleas for families,
only the wail of a bagpipe echoes throughout the valley.

Born of Americans, yet . . .

Shamrocks and thistles, leprechauns and faeries, druids
and clans, myths and legends create a patchwork uniquely me.

Ahern – Ball
O'Herron – Ballantyne

My name is mine.
It is, always will be, my own.
Even after change and change and change
through family history:

I cannot – I will not – hide behind a word,
a fear, a banner of cloth. I am me – freckles and all.

I am not simply white.

Born of Americans,
my spirit danced with the wind over the ocean
generations ago to plunge –
not in a melting pot of opportunity or in the Promised
Land of milk and honey, but in a sea of inhumanity –
crawling and gasping for air, clawing and struggling to survive.

The hope I have is what I have made of it –
like my mother and father before me.

The Factory, Canal Street
New York 1901

Eyes adjust
to needle and thread;
from corner to corner,
a graveyard of girls
dusted with lint –
pennies for a twelve-hour day;
whistle raising the dead

and the immigrant breaks
the back of his brother

Sew another sleeve, a collar
cut the string –
revolution on the streets
without bullets or men

and the immigrant breaks
the back of his sister

sailing from green encircled
by sea, their road stopped
in a room enclosed
like a tomb
with the clatter and clack
of treadles –
a rumbling tumult of hell

Bertie Ryan

Even in sepia her porcelain skin gleams,
and I can imagine her brogue, full of music.
One moment snapped her secret

smile – what else does she hide?
Besides a lover, I mean. The one who sailed
from green shores with her. Or did she meet

him in this new world? The Promised Land.
Narrow streets gutted with dirt, piss. Rising
to local fame with smoke and noise in dance

halls, did she leave him? Or was it all too much
till he left her? Did he know about their daughter
– abandoned, handled like a maid?

No roots to transplant, a Kerry lily birthed
an American beauty. Did she bloom, fade,
wither? This lone picture leaves no answers.

If I had known her, what would she have said?

Fountainhead

Around the corner waves crash into cliffs then rush
like a waterfall back to the sea – forever chasing
its source. Gulls overhead sound like children
arguing, and once more I'm in the streets
of Limericktown – clouds suddenly drawn
over this bright day.

Fighting for place,
fighting for power, fighting for peace in a family
too large, a house too small, and dreams bigger
than anyone could expect to come true. Wind
kicks up froths of white atop the turquoise sea,
and melancholy recedes, leaving just the gulls and me.

Deora De

Her arms outstretched in mist
and silence, Saint Brigid, protector
of women, smiles as I cross
the cobbled stones.

Deora de
masks the darkened archway
that's hard to see except
for burgeoning red buds.

I'm startled by the gloom. Air musty,
a damp rust odor where water drips,
stains walls, letters, votives, beads
and photos.
Faces fade from black
and white to sepia. One candle shivers.

Where is she who opened her cloak
to clothe the land, green as far as fields
surge to the sea?

Kneeling, I dip my fingers
in the pool and sign the cross.

Homecoming

Celtic crosses break the green,
green fields rolling before me.
The sea cradles red and black
fishing boats, curlews dance
over white-tipped waves.

Pink and yellow store-fronts
in Kilkenny shout *Paddy's Restaurant*,
O'Flaherty's Chemists. Umbrellas
and caps disappear behind doors
on the brown and gray streets,
violas, impatiens, pansies bob
in window boxes cheering the dark.

Gray limestone frames thatched
cottages, rock stretching across
the Burren. Buses wind around stone
fences guarding patches of grass.

Wind rushes through Moll's Gap,
tosses horses' manes and ruffles
the wooly sheep. Castle ruins shade
Kerry cows in the valley below, black
dotting the green. Step between two
sheltering knolls, the silence is louder
than the wind above.

I am home.
This wind-swept patch of dirt and rock
envelopes and embraces me.
It claims me as its own.

And they do speak.

Kilmacduagh

The ghosts still walk at Kilmaduagh
in daylight and the dark,
so be careful if you go there
for it's bound to leave its mark.

Visitors say it's the wind that moans
but locals there know better;
though bodies lie beneath the earth
the soul is still unfettered.

The doorless watchtower soars
above markers in the ground;
ruins stretch across the field
and mountains hover, spellbound.

Cows now roam at will there
where once an altar stood,
though remarkably not breaking
the reverential mood.

And if you stand quite silent
among those stones of gray,
you're bound to hear the whispers
of the penitent left to pray.

So take your time when wandering
through gravestones fallen and upright,
but when the trees begin to stir
don't depend upon your sight.

The ghosts still walk at Kilmacduagh
in daylight and the dark,
just be careful who you take there
for it will surely leave its mark.

The Gloaming

Holy well and faerie tree stand
in the lengthening shadows,
and thrushes sing an evensong.

The stones of this sacred place suffered
knees of sinners, prayers of saints
muffled through leafy grotto, begging
forgiveness or, at least, forgetfulness.

Worn course around the white-thorn
witnessed generations of pilgrims
who grasped after miracles spiked
on branches in a cobweb of ribbon and cloth.

Once, worshippers shifted stone
to build cairns, avoid the faeries' caul.
The veil lifts, *sugat* intoning,
In the name of the Father, the Son,
the Holy Ghost – water, tree and rock
blessed to Saint Michael. Sign the cross.
Now Sunday's sanctuary lies empty.

Thrush choir quiets while white blossoms
gather at vespers of day, wrinkle the water's surface.

Tranquility, the Aran Ferry

Eyes slit against sparkling sun,
lulled by engine and slap of waves,
I spot a solitary shag paddle
portside as the ferry heads to Inis
Mór. A flock of herring gulls feed
off starboard like pigeons in a park.
Tourists talk and snap photos.
Islanders settle packages and bums
inside, shun the hype. Wind whips
up froth – the wake behind us swells,
sea like an icing-covered cake.

An Rún

And sometime take the time to drive out west
Into County Clare, along the Flaggy Shore,
In September or October, when the wind
And the light are working off each other.
– Seamus Heaney, "Postscript"

Sunlight settles in the west
across the conversation of the waves.
Red and orange swirl the sky, slide
into the shifting sea. Connemara
greets this water with a stony shore,
a deceptive monochrome of slate.

But in the secret, in the quiet,
fairy thimbles purple the gray
Burren, snuggle into crevices.
They thrust through cracks, carpeting
stone in a tapestry of periwinkle,
lavender, violet. Gathered at midnight
in the early dew, this foxglove
is *méaracán sí* – strength to restore
the health, the blood – vitality.

Orchids pink and maidenhair
ferns emerge from this granite bed.
Swayed by riffs of air above
and spurts of water below,
they flourish in these parts.

Below this rocky surface lies
a whispering stream of life.
Nearby lakes drift to the Burren,
sink into fissured limestone
and wander to the ocean
where sunlight settles, westering.

Inís Oírr

Tobar Einne awaits –
my lips bruised with trouble,
tongue tumbles in prayer.
Dip fingers in water clear
and cold, sign the cross.

This side of the island empty
save wind and sun sweeping
over fields of stone, grass.

Surely Saint Enda hears.

Inisheer

Strips of potatoes nestle near Paints
prancing. Cows graze close in fields
empty of all but grass. Inishmaan
lies close with none but these to relish
the sun sliding into water beyond.

Red, yellow, pink, even shell houses
overlook the harbour – bright colors,
shine to cheer dreary days. Beyond,
a graveyard of black and white marble
sinks quietly to rest.

Daisies dance at roadside edge.
Picking one, I think of you. Here
they sprout beside fences, cottages,
ruins. Tufts of white and gold glow.

Knockeven, County Clare

Wave follows wave as fog and shadow
struggle to gain control of the gray
sky stretched before me. Rain pings
the windows where marsh
marigolds wave wildly in the field.
Two horses nibble grass, and the wind
doesn't bother them, cause them to turn
from their plans, their day – unlike me.
Driven indoors by this sudden cold front,
huddled in a corner under blankets
like an escaped fugitive, I wile away
the day in a cocoon of warmth, light.
Lured by printed pages, I'm oblivious
to nature's battle beyond the glass.

McGann's Pub, Doolin

– A break in the music, and I push past
tourists slanting against the scarred bar
until I spot Mick. He nods me to a corner,
swapping his fiddle for a half-finished
pint on his way over. Just back from Nepal,
with a kiss for each cheek and a *How've ye*
been? he slouches next to me, launches
yarns of mountains and snow and a yak
that ran off with his gear.

I wait
for the story of the other woman I'd heard
already from friends. It could have been
me. It was me. What about the *other*
other woman? That's the story I don't get
in the smoke and stout-filled air. Laughter,
glasses clinking backdrop to the tin whistle,
the bodhrán that gluts my body, my blood.

He heads for the fiddle again, tunnels through
the crowd savoring the *craic*. Pipes, drums,
strings swell the air, drown the natter.
The other players welcome him back to the circle
as though he'd never left, like no hole had ever appeared.

Hag's Head

O'Brien's Tower heaved with tourists, talk,
so along the edge of the Cliffs I walked
listening to roaring waves and seagulls' call.
Pushed by wind, called by tidal flow –
blue sky above, black sea below –
the farther I tramp, the fewer people I see.

Farmers toil in a Liscannor field
while I search for what the Cliffs won't reveal
except to the rocks and the wind and the sea.

Traveling People, County Galway

These outsiders belong to lands of lemons, sands.
They shiver in this Irish mist, this moist and rocky
realm, home to paler kings.

Reds and yellows, under putty skies,
stripe their stalls in the marketplace –
the tinkers' hammers ping, metals gleam.
Dark hair, dark eyes calloused to our sun.
Women lined, bent with shawls and scarves,
tell fortunes for a bit of copper coin or gold.

Born foreign to our world, they look for roots,
trace their routes, over and over again
along this Burren road where little grows.
Every year we watch them come and watch them go,
and keep our children clear.

Across the Bay
Knockeven, County Clare

Lights from Lahinch glimmer
by the beach far below my window.
Safe in this field, in this house

far from others, the wind whirrs,
rattles past my windows;
the sea moans through the night.

I close my eyes and, even now,
snugged between cool sheets,
I feel the suck of surf, waves stampede

my ankles: I see my life, foundering.
Defenses built layer after layer
erode like sand rushing out to sea.

Grass rustles and trees thrash
in the growing storm. The lights
of Lahinch shine an ocean away.

Rising Tide

Gray and gritty with grime,
Limericktown crouches beneath
a cold Spring sky. Families
huddle round smoking fires
and rain pours ever down,
transforming streets to streams.
Tonight I sit and wait:
for you to come, for life to change.

I watch damp settle into the walls,
drip through the ceiling.
I must move or rot.
Time won't tarry though I sit still –
the sand sinks ever down, trickling
like the drops down my window.

Montage

June
farmers bale hay
roll after roll stored in fields
black, plastic-wrapped corpses
of summer growth – bones
ready to pick clean come
winter

Gray granite ruins shadow the field,
a tribute to glory days of stone
when the price of a slab was worth
a man's life. Now the quarry
stands in stony silence, decomposing,
a corpse above ground.

Patterns of stone lie over the land
walls built less to divide than to unburden
the ground. Dismal clouds menace green
fields. Who would believe it's midsummer's
day when mist and chill cocoon us indoors?

Fog blurs every sharp cliff edge;
furze and foxglove glimmer
this dark day. Mist brushes
my face, cleansing. Tourists want
the superficial Moher, have no time
to waste, to give. So I walk alone
along the Cliffs, waiting for the world
beyond my sight to draw me in.

Blue peeks from layers of white, gray,
fog drawing back from the watery sun.
Pinpricks of silver shimmer across the sea –
another day above Liscannor.

The Skelligs

Rock rises from the ocean surface,
waves shock and break the base –
mouth of hell leading to heaven's
heights. The pilgrim struggles up,
crossing Christ's Saddle to pass
through the Needle's Eye. Here the monks
withdrew, stacked slab upon slab
until the huts secured their hermitage.

Solitary from *samhain* to spring, even the gods
found solace among moss and meadowgrass,
toad rush and chickweed. Sea pinks dawn
the *imbolc*; puffins paddle offshore then join
gossiping kittiwakes. Gannets settle like sea foam
across the jagged stone, and the Washerwomen
tiptoe back from the west.

Vortex

I know the dead can wait,
but what about the living?

Holding on is perilous.
Dragged down by the undertow,
I grasp at phantoms that tarry
at the edge of dusk.
I find myself in the middle of
                                        silence,
a stillness I've never known.
But my breath fragments this illusion
of order, my heartbeat counts
time skidding away.

Letting go isn't as easy
as it sounds – like bread scattered
over peaked waves or balloons
circling in the breeze; a moment
that lingers, hovers for one brief
breath. A gradual loosening
of the hand, the soul.

Glossary

ailim:	elm
An Górta Mór:	The Great Hunger
Beal Na mBlath:	Mouth of Flowers
Big Fella:	Michael Collins
bodhrán:	hand-held goat skin drum
Brú na Bóinne:	Boyne Palace
Burren:	rocky, karst area in County Claire, the west of Ireland
Carolan:	17th/18th century harpist/bard
craic:	fun; friendly gathering
deora de:	a red flower; the name means "Tears of God"
Éire:	another name for Ireland
ficheall:	chess
Formorians:	sea pirates, sometimes said to be giants
Imbolc:	the beginning of Spring
méaracán sí:	fairy thimble; a type of foxglove supposed to provide good health
Paints:	a type of horse
Rosaleen:	another name for Ireland
Samhain:	All Hallow's Eve
scalpeen:	lean-to shelter made from the remains of a former home
sí, sídhe:	fairies; fairy mounds
Skelligs:	an island off the coast of Kerry which houses an early Celtic monastery
sugat:	priest
Tír na Nóg:	Land of Eternal Youth and Beauty; the Golden Shore
Tobar Einne:	The Well of Einne

About the Author

KB Ballentine teaches English and theatre arts to high school and college students when she's not writing. She has attended writing academies in both America and Britain. Published in *Bent Pin, MO: Writings from the River*, *Sequoia Review*, *Apocalypse* and *Touchstone*, she shares her work in various poetry groups. In 2006 she was a finalist for the Joy Harjo Poetry Award and in 2007 was awarded a prize from the Dorothy Sargent Rosenberg Memorial Fund. KB has a B.A. and M.A. in Writing and a MFA in Creative Writing and Poetry.

About the Book

The titles and subtitles are set in Celtic, with the text of the poems in Georgia. The paper is 55 lbs with a 10 pt laminated cover. Interior design and cover by Greyhound Books.
The cover photograph features a stone wall in the Mourne Mountains, Northern Ireland between the Bloody Bridge and the Silent Valley. All photographs by Jim Johnston except back cover photograph of the author, which was taken by Janie Sheldon.

About Celtic Cat Publishing

Celtic Cat Publishing was founded in 1995 to publish emerging and established writers.

The following works are available from Celtic Cat Publishing at www.celticcatpublishing.com, from Amazon.com and from major bookstores.

Poetry

Exile: Poems of an Irish Immigrant, James B. Johnston

Marginal Notes, Frank Jamison

Rough Ascension and Other Poems of Science, Arthur J. Stewart

Bushido: The Virtues of Rei and Makoto, Arthur J. Stewart

Ebbing & Flowing Springs: New and Selected Poems and Prose (1976-2001), Jeff Daniel Marion

Humor

My Barbie Was an Amputee, Angie Vicars

Chanukah

One for Each Night: Chanukah Tales and Recipes, Marilyn Kallet

www.ingramcontent.com/pod-product-compliance
Lightning Source LLC
LaVergne TN
LVHW020651100826
845148LV00012B/2431

* 9 7 8 0 9 6 5 8 9 5 0 9 5 *